W9-CFC-606

HAIR-RAISING HALLOWEEN

MAKE FRIGHTFUL PROPS

DIY EYEBALLS, ORGANS, AND MORE

by Mary Meinking

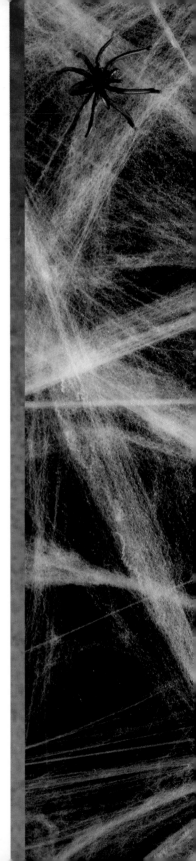

Blazers Books are published by Capstone Press,
1710 Roe Crest Drive, North Mankato, Minnesota 56003
www.mycapstone.com

Library of Congress Cataloging-in-Publication data
Library of Congress Cataloging-in-Publication data is available on the
Library of Congress website.
ISBN 978-1-5435-3031-5 (library binding)
ISBN 978-1-5435-3035-3 (paperback)
ISBN 978-1-5435-3089-6 (eBook PDF)

Editorial Credits
Mandy Robbins, editor; Juliette Peters, designer; Morgan Walters,
media researcher; Laura Manthe, production specialist; Marcy Morin,
scheduler; Sarah Schuette, photo stylist

Photo Credits
All images Capstone Studio: Karon Dubke.
Shutterstock: Sasa Prudkov, cover, design element throughout,
Wandeaw, cover, design element throughout

Printed and bound in the United States of America.
PA017

Table of Contents

NIGHTMARE MAKERS

Do you want to creep out even your bravest friends? Make an eye-popping eyeball or a shocking shrunken head. Everyone will be freaked out at your gross collection.

GLOWING MUMMY'S HAND

This eerie mummy's hand just crept out of the tomb. Watch out so it doesn't grab you!

1. Fill the fingers and palm of the glove with stuffing.

2. Have an adult cut the neck off the bottle.

3. Stretch the glove over the bottom of the bottle. Tape it in place.

4. Wrap the gauze up the arm, and around the hand and each finger. Overlap as you go.

5. Place a glow stick inside the arm to display.

Freaky Fact:

The ancient Egyptians didn't just turn people into mummies. They mummified their pets too!

self-adherent—describes something that sticks to itself

GORY BLOOD

Halloween isn't the same without gory blood. Make the perfect fake blood to accent your gross decor.

WHAT YOU NEED:

- ❏ water
- ❏ light corn syrup
- ❏ red food coloring
- ❏ green food coloring
- ❏ powdered hot cocoa mix
- ❏ a plastic bowl
- ❏ a spoon

1. For runny blood to splatter on things, mix:

- ❏ 2 tablespoons (30 milliliters) of water
- ❏ 2 tablespoons (30 mL) of corn syrup
- ❏ 4 drops of red coloring
- ❏ 1 drop of green coloring

2. For thicker blood mix:

- ❏ 2 tablespoons (30 mL) of corn syrup
- ❏ 2 drops of red coloring
- ❏ ¼ cup (60 mL) cocoa mix

*Fake blood is safe to eat. It will last months if stored in a sealed container.

Tip:

Be careful. Food coloring stains! It's difficult to get out of clothing, furniture, or carpet.

OOZING BRAIN

Do you want to look like a mad scientist? Put this realistic brain on display.

1. Wad the newspapers into a 6-inch (15-cm) long oval shape with a flat bottom. Wrap it with duct tape.

2. Roll the clay into long ropes.

3. Spray the top of your duct-taped form with glue.

4. Wind the clay ropes over half of the form. Repeat on the other side. Let it dry overnight.

5. Paint the brain white. Leave the cracks and gaps red. Let it dry.

6. Place the brain on the platter. Drizzle with fake blood.

Freaky Fact:

In France in the 1890s, haunted house fake blood was made from cooked insects. Early black-and-white movies used chocolate syrup for fake blood.

HEAD HUNTER

Hundreds of years ago, South American warriors used to shrink their victims' heads. Make your own shrunken head on a stick to terrify your friends and family.

WHAT YOU NEED:

- ❏ air-dry clay (any color)
- ❏ a foam head or skull
- ❏ industrial-strength glue
- ❏ acrylic paint (light brown and dark brown)
- ❏ a paintbrush
- ❏ fake hair
- ❏ tan twine
- ❏ a scissors
- ❏ a stick

1. Use the clay to sculpt eyes, brows, a nose, and teeth on the foam head. Once dry, glue the clay down.

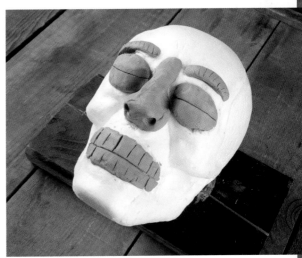

Continued on next page

2. Paint the entire head dark brown. Let it dry. Lightly brush on light brown paint. Leave it dark in the cracks. Let it dry.

3. Glue the hair to the **scalp**.

scalp—the skin that covers the top of the head where hair grows

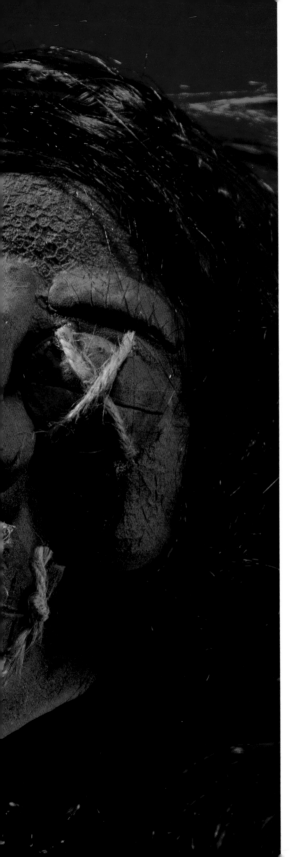

4. Cut 4 small pieces of twine. Glue an "X" over each eye.

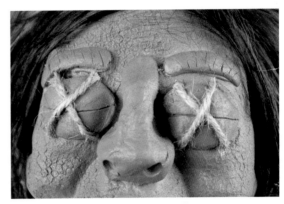

5. Cut 4 more small pieces of twine. Tie a knot in the middle of each one. Glue the twine over the lips. Let it dry.

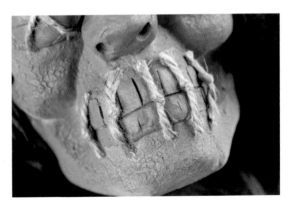

6. Once everything is dry, gently poke the stick through the bottom.

PLUCKED EYEBALL

Up close, eyeballs are gross. They're even gorier plucked from their **sockets**.

1. Cut a piece of yarn 3 inches (8 cm) long. Unravel one end of the yarn halfway.

2. Spread out the fibers around the table tennis ball. Glue them down. Leave the yarn tail.

3. Cut out the iris. Glue it over the center of the fibers. Let it dry.

4. Paint the ball with nail polish. Let it dry.

WHAT YOU NEED:

❏ a scissors
❏ dark red yarn
❏ a table tennis ball
❏ school glue
❏ a life-sized eye **iris** cut out of a magazine or printed in color
❏ clear nail polish

Tip:

Use creepy props to display your eyeballs. Set a few in a dismembered hand. Have one falling out of a mask's eye socket.

socket—a hole or hollow place where something fits in

iris—the round, colored part of an eye

HEAD IN A JAR

Did someone lose his head?
This ghastly sight will freak out your visitors.

WHAT YOU NEED:

- ❏ a color copier with white, letter-size paper
- ❏ a scissors
- ❏ white glue
- ❏ fake hair
- ❏ a large, clear jar with a lid
- ❏ fake blood (optional)

1. Put your color copier on the **high-resolution** setting.

2. Open the lid to the copier. Place your ear on the glass where it starts copying. Close your eyes.

3. Start the copier. Press and roll your face along the copier light as it moves across the glass.

4. Cut off the white edges of the paper copy.

5. Glue the hair around the face of the copy. Let it dry.

high-resolution—having the capability to produce images with fine detail

Continued on next page

6. Place the picture inside the jar. Press to the outside edges.

7. (Optional) Drip fake blood on the face and in the bottom of the jar. Put on the lid with some hair poking out.

GIANT CREEPY SPIDER

This is no itsy bitsy spider. It is what nightmares are made of!

WHAT YOU NEED:

- ❏ black acrylic paint
- ❏ paintbrush
- ❏ a 5-inch (13-cm) foam ball
- ❏ an 8-inch (21-cm) foam ball
- ❏ industrial-strength glue
- ❏ black sculpting clay
- ❏ 8 red plastic jewels
- ❏ eight 12-inch (30.5-cm) pieces of bendable black **garland**

1. Paint both foam balls with black paint. Let them dry.

2. Glue the balls together. Let them dry.

3. Use clay to fill in any space between the two balls.

4. Glue the jewels on the small ball where the spider's eyes would be. Let them dry.

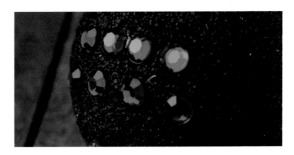

garland—a rope made from leaves, flowers, or other items, such as an artificial pine branch

Continued on next page

5. Use clay to form the pincher fangs on the small ball. Let them dry. Glue them below the eyes.

6. Bend the garland pieces into "L" shapes. Stick four per side into the balls. Fan out the legs.

Freaky Fact:

The world's largest spider is the goliath bird-eating **tarantula**. Its body is 12 inches (30.5 cm) long. It has 1-inch (2.5-cm) long fangs.

tarantula—a large, hairy spider

CREEPY CAGED GOBLIN

Keep this creepy goblin trapped in its cage. Otherwise, you might need to sleep with one eye open.

WHAT YOU NEED:

- ❏ an old doll
- ❏ a scissors
- ❏ fake eyeballs
- ❏ sculpting clay
- ❏ acrylic paints in green, black, red, and **iridescent**
- ❏ 3 paintbrushes
- ❏ 2 small round laundry baskets
- ❏ metallic colored spray paint
- ❏ industrial-strength glue

1. Rough up your doll. Cut up its clothes or add dirt smudges and blood to them.

2. Stick the eyeballs on the doll with clay. Let it dry.

3. Paint the doll green except for its eyes and hair. Let it dry.

4. Lightly brush on iridescent paint. Leave green in cracks. Let it dry.

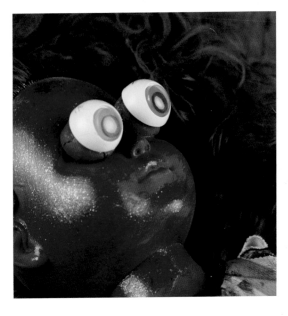

iridescent—describes material that displays many colors for a rainbow effect

Continued on next page

5. Paint the mouth and inside of ears a combination of red and black. Give your goblin a dark, ugly single eyebrow.

6. Have an adult spray paint the laundry baskets. Let them dry.

7. Place your goblin in a laundry basket. Glue the other basket over it. Let it dry.

8. Get creative and add some creepy touches! Drape moss or cobwebs on your cage.

GLOSSARY

dismembered (diss-MEM-burd)–describes something that is detached from the rest of itself

garland (GAR-luhnd)–a rope made from leaves, flowers, or other items, such as an artificial pine branch

high-resolution (HI rez-uh-LOO-shuhn)–having the capability to produce images with fine detail

iridescent (ir-uh-DESS-uhnt)–describes material that displays many colors for a rainbow effect

iris (EYE-riss)–the round, colored part of an eye

scalp (SKALP)–the skin that covers the top of the head where hair grows

self-adherent (SELF ad-HERE-uhnt)–describes something that sticks to itself

socket (SOK-it)–a hole or hollow place where something fits in

tarantula (tuh-RAN-chuh-luh)–a large, hairy spider

READ MORE

Loh-Hagan, Virginia. *Haunted House. D.I.Y. Make it Happen.* Ann Arbor, Mich.: Cherry Lake Publishing, 2016.

Owen, Ruth. *I Can Throw a Party*. Kids Can Do It! New York: Windmill Books, 2017.

Owen, Ruth. *The Halloween Gross-Out Guide. DIY for Boys.* New York: PowerKids Press, 2014.

INTERNET SITES

Use FactHound to find Internet sites related to this book.

Visit *www.facthound.com*

Just type in 9781543530315 and go!

Check out projects, games and lots more at
www.capstonekids.com

INDEX